Like a Bird above a Flooded Land

Hendrick Ferguson

Like a Bird above a Flooded Land

A Collection of Musings & Maxims

Los Angeles ∎ Miami ∎ New York

Palm Springs Publishing
Los Angeles ∎ Miami ∎ New York

Cover Design by Hendrick Ferguson

Twitter Handle: @unchainedthinkr
Facebook: Hendrick Ferguson

Produced in the United States of America

ISBN-13: 978 0 9742949 4 0

©2019 by Hendrick Ferguson

Notice

All rights reserved. No part of this publication maybe reproduced or transmitted in any form or by any means, electronic or mechanical, including photocopying, recording, or any other information storage and retrieval system, without the written permission of the author.

For Kathleen Taylor

To the deluded dreamers, sovereign soldiers, singular souls, spotless spirits, truth travelers, passion pushers, and titillating thinkers, this book is an ode to you; soar at your own altitude.

In recognition of my patrons

To Ben Carlsen: for providing me with an extra pair of eyes and helping me to tidy up the material for publication. To the Toronto Reference Library for providing me with access to the best research facility any writer could hope for.

IN THE INTERIOR

thirteen | A brief presentation of this selection

Part One

seventeen | Sorted Musings & Maxims
nineteen | Soul Goals
twenty-three | True Triumph
twenty-seven | Staying Power
thirty-one | Speak Your Piece
thirty-five | Politics & Justice
fifty-three | Heart Facts
fifty-five | Verses for Humanity
fifty-seven | Self-Notes

Part Two

sixty-one | Unsorted Musings & Maxims
one hundred and seven | Parting Words
one hundred and nine | Notes & Sources

A brief presentation of this selection

This book is my delicate attempt to remain creatively engaged, if only to a fragmented degree, in the midst of an artistically desolate period; whereby I've been indisposed due to a series of external events which have impaired my ability to write for an extended interval. This lack of activity and inspiration in turn, has plunged me into the uninhabited realm of creative insolvency.

For many writers life's unforeseen tempests are undiscovered gold quarries that are just waiting to be mined, and life's gloomy intermissions are usually a time of creative profitability.

For me, contrary to that writing principle, disquieting times can stir up a hornet's nest of creative inactivity, depending on the nature of the situation.

There's also that undeniable notion that trials and tribulations lend themselves to the creative process, i.e. it provides the raw material for the endeavor, which I don't necessarily diverge from lock, stock and barrel. Even so, I am of the view that before one can make any meaningful use of a traumatic condition it needs to be properly aged and distilled.

As I write this I am living through the most supervening event of my life; I am being openly violated and subjugated in a country that was meant to offer me some respite from being persecuted in the country of my birth, but instead added to my burden tenfold. And it has been equally as disruptive as it has been destructive.

To compensate for this sustained interruption in my creative productivity, and desperately seeking even the tiniest bit of inspiration, or creative lifesaver of any sort, I jumped to a chat in my mind that I had with a fellow artist friend of mine.

She had suggested that I create a book out of my assortment of musings and maxims; in the belief that it would shake me out of my creative funk.

My initial reaction to her suggestion was it is far too derivative and lacking in real creativity. But then, over the years I would be in conversation with other folks and they would express the same desire for me to make a collection of my aphorisms available in a book.

Many of these musings, as well as maxims, range from bites of social discourse, political matters, morsels of philosophical perspectives, and waxing about romantic associations.

This book is essentially a compilation of random spells of inspiration — and revulsion — extracted from a life in exile.

— Hendrick Ferguson

Part One

Sorted Musings & Maxims

—Soul Goals—

I

To dream is to aspire to fulfill one's soul desires: to satisfy a yearning, to speak a truth, to follow a predestined path. It's all these things and more. Dreams are not definitive in their desires. Instead, they are infinite in their possibilities. Dreams don't exist below the surface. They live above the skies. Therefore, it requires extending yourself, and reaching forth, in order to attain your goals.

II

There are numerous beneficiaries of a dream, but only one principal investor — and that's you.

III

Dreams must be allowed to roam free, uninhibited by boundaries or consequences, if they are to survive.

IV

One who dreams has a dictatorial and benevolent ruler that resides inside of them, governing their path in a sort of cult like manner.

V

In the universe of dreams, when you gamble and lose, you risk losing yourself. Dreams can be a very costly proposition for a dreamer.

VI

Don't permit any critic to override your vision of your dream. It's your trek and don't let anyone else direct your path.

VII

It's one or the other: artists either produce abundantly or perish in the pits of creative drought. That is the fate of all artists – and there are no in-betweens. This is a result of both internal as well as external circumstances.

—True Triumph—

I

No path to success is without its rugged terrain.

II

Your failures don't necessarily speak to your abilities. While others may be in the position to judge your work, ultimately honing your craft and striving for excellence is what makes you great. Success is all relative.

III

Following the Money vs. Following your Dream

No amount of money or success can compensate for not following your dream. Your aspiration is your soul-fulfilling desire. Success, on the other hand, is commonly gauged by the amount of money you accumulate, and to what extent you are lauded by society. However, as long as you're doing something that furnishes your zeal for life, that's all that matters. Fulfilling your soul's desires is more gratifying than money or any accolade designed to acknowledge your talent.

IV

What really determines the success of a venture? Is it merely completing a project and getting the result you'd hoped for, or is it more about societal measurements? That is, the achievement of wealth, fame, and the approval of others. Can a project completed satisfactorily be unsuccessful? Yes! And, just as easily, an incomplete project can be successful. The ultimate goal, of course, would be to have both a satisfactory completion as well as to be lauded by others. However, the one opinion that should always matter the most is your own.

—Staying Power—

I

We should never view rejection as defeat, but instead it should be seen as a timely delay.

II

Though it may be of little or no consolation to the uncelebrated person, I believe all great works are rewarded in the end, however belated — sometimes even in death.

III

It's said that the more you ask of life, the more life demands of you. And it's true. Once you've grasped this concept, instead of viewing your challenges as a burden, you will see them as an agreement between you and your desires. The satisfaction will then come from you living up to your part of the bargain — which requires working your ass off. Everything else is a matter of timing.

IV

For some, the slightest hint of an "ill wind" will blow them away. That's because when you don't have sufficient commitment, you will always be subject to the vagaries of life, and the harsh judgments of others.

V

When a boxer receives a blow to the head from his opponent and he falls helplessly to the floor, it's not the might of the punch that will defeat him, but rather his willingness to get back up before the referee counts to ten. That is what ultimately determines whether a boxer wins or loses. Rejection and setbacks must be viewed the same way. How you react to the action is far more significant than the action itself.

VI

Never concentrate on someone's current place in life. It's all temporary. Being victorious isn't a permanent state, and neither is failure. Rises and falls are proverbial.

VII

Disappointment should never be allowed to rule our world, nor should it discourage you from your dreams. More than abilities, being victorious requires your drive to succeed in spite of obstacles and challenges.

VIII

Failure has been a temporary visitor to everyone who has ever succeeded in life.

—Speak Your Piece—

I

Incessantly bemoaning the *weather condition (or whatever trivialities) can justifiably be considered as complaining too much. On the other hand, speaking* out against any form of injustice, no matter how often it's done – or how small/large the infraction, is admirable, and should never be confused with petty grousing.

II

The same courts that convict guilty people are identical to the ones that imprison innocent folks. The judicial system is not an exact science. It is therefore important for us to mind our judgment of persons who have been declared responsible for criminal offences.

III

Subjugation: The trick is…

The trick is to get you to consent to substandard treatment.
The trick is to drill into you that you are nothing special.
The trick is to seek out and inflame your insecurities.
The trick is to belittle you constantly and unexpectedly.
The trick is to sabotage your efforts and label you a loser.

Once they've succeeded in priming you, conditioning you, and brainwashing you — they now have you completely under their thumb. And like the dog in Pavlov's experiments, it's not even necessary for them to supply you with scraps of meat in order to get you to acquiesce to their commands.

IV

Every artist, if they are true to what the word "artist" infers, is an activist by default. The visual artist dissents through his/her paintings; the singer through his/her songs; the writer through his/her writings — and so forth.

V

There's zero nobility in holding a belief without the required amount of conviction to withstand the opposing force.

—Politics & Justice—

I

Society is at fault for corrupt government officials because we tolerate them. Even though we are keen to say "it's our country" and "they work for us," and all that jazz. However, as soon as they fuck-up, and no matter how catastrophic, we do nothing at all. Instead we revert back to an infantile state, throw our hands up in the air and cry out, "what can we do?"

II

Government propaganda, like all artificial, manipulative mind feed, is intended to have an air of probability. However, it's nothing more than half-truths adulterated with lies, counterfeited facts, if you will. All manufactured to defraud you of your sense of reasoning and to deactivate your conscience, whilst reformatting your thoughts.

III

The concoctions of lies and loftier promises served up by politicians are capable of leaving any man or woman drunk with misunderstanding.

IV

A corrupt government has no heart; it's just a soulless entity that's more machinery than human. It's unfortunate that people need to be reminded of this. The fact is they will sacrifice any one of us if we become an inconvenient liability for them.

V

In every instance that we cower and run off with our tails tucked between our legs, we're telling the system it's okay to violate and deprive us of our rights and dignity. If we don't have the conviction to see justice through to maturity, we will be repaid with more injustice.

VI

If a government is corrupt, you can replace it. However, if the people are of the same persuasion… all bets are off.

VII

You've not been properly persecuted until you've been victimized by all branches of a government.

VIII

Once a government has dug themselves a hole (one that's 6 ft deep, to be exact) they are usually on the hunt for a body — a specific somebody — preferably a dead body.

IX

Make sure mister politician has un-forked his tongue before you permit him/her to address you.

X

The key to a well-functioning democracy is the electorate must maintain the same fervor they displayed during the electoral process, if they hope to keep elected officials accountable.

XI

Any country that's more concerned with controlling its citizens than seeing that justice is being dispensed is only free in theory.

XII

In a collectivist society one's mind is community property by virtue of unrelenting conditioning by the government. As a consequence, one's conscience is governed by an agreed upon consensus.

XIII

Silence is like the fertilizer that nurtures incidents of injustice and allows it to grow. And corrupt politicians are like the farmers that use it as manure to cultivate more corruption.

XIV

Overzealous folks in authority will accuse you of any and everything their frail minds can concoct; completely ignoring good conscience and evidence of any kind, in favor of their misguided sense of superiority.

XV

What does a compromised government do in cases where they're liable? They create alternative issues of lesser value that they are willing to remedy, and employ straw-man tactics to disarm and confuse the victim.

XVI

Politics is a crop field of low lying fruits, and many politicians are spoiled rotten like those fruits at the foot of the tree.

XVII

Propaganda is like medicine; mind altering medication that's intended to influence your thoughts, by using counterfeit facts. For that reason it needs to be administered in the same manner as prescribed drugs; in sufficient dosages and at regular intervals.

XVIII

The scales of justice are unbalanced because too many people cower in the face of big bad governments. And yet we're astonished as to why injustice is so prevalent in society.

The state is very adamant about pursuance of the law when any of us breach it, but when the infraction is in the reverse order, suddenly the rules becomes the exception.

XIX

The violations against us as human beings that we foolishly discount today eventually become the ghost that returns to haunt us tomorrow. And that isn't mere speculative musing.

No thinking person can deny that all of our present-day entanglements are a sum total of our unresolved experience — debris from current, as well as, previous storms, if you will.

For as we know future events have no ability to affect our present-day state of affairs, one way or the other. This much is a fact. Again, it's only our past and existing trials that have the clout to turn our universe topsy-turvy.

With the previously mentioned rationale in mind, we must be mindful not to give implicit orders to have our lives directed by others, lest we care to live by the whim of an unjust system.

XX

It's reasonable to conclude that most people don't hold ill feelings towards police officers, and the ones that do, are inclined to be folks who feel as if they were betrayed and wronged by those in law enforcement.

XXI

There comes a time when we are obligated by principle, to stand up against injustice. Or we risk contributing to systemic evils that in time will boomerang right back to us.

The reason for this is simple: when acts of injustice are allowed to go repeatedly unchecked it leads to normalization of such conduct, which in turn distorts our collective internal sense of what's just and unjust. Further, it ends up making sacrificial lambs out of the majority for a select minority.

It's therefore imperative as a society, that we are disposed to ensure that real justice is being rendered at all times, and in those cases where it's been perverted, it's vital that corrections are made, lest we have no right to regard ourselves as a just society.

XXII

When most people think of an authoritarian state their minds quickly race to countries that are governed by dictators. But that's just the most common type of authoritarian ruled societies. There's another less known breed and that's those of a "third force" variety. What's a third force form of totalitarian rule? That's when the security apparatus of any given country holds more power than the elected officials, and therefore by default becomes the de facto leader.

XXIII

A true leader doesn't reflect the barren values of his/her populace, and he/she certainly doesn't make criminally designed pacts with them.

XXIV

No matter what country you reside in, if you happen to file a police complaint, it will only be dealt with if it's an inconsequential matter. Any incident that requires disciplinary action (of any sort) against police misconduct will be ignored and/or covered-up, to be sure. As if that wasn't bad enough, the complainant can also expect to be harassed, threatened, demonized, slandered, stigmatized, have his/her civil rights trampled on, and falsely accused/investigated for everything under the sun and the moon. The objective is to bury the truth by any means necessary.

XXV

A great leader inspires his/her citizens and offers hope in times of strife. The aforesaid is a recognized adage, so it's not as though the idea being trumpeted is a new one. In stark contrast to the previous point, a despot posing as a "virtuous leader," will manipulate his/her citizens whilst instilling fear and compliance in them. Again, there's nothing novel about the latter concept, and even a person with only a marginal sense of history can bear witness to this.

XXVI

Sometimes a government just needs to own up to its misdeeds, instead of using the proverbial method of "attack and destroy" to silence a person whom they've victimized (or they are oppressing) with further acts of victimization. Fire will not extinguish fire.

XXVII

Without political moxie, it doesn't take very long before the new leader starts to resemble the old one.

XXVIII

We're not supposed to still be here as a society, when free and law abiding men and women, are openly violated for voicing an opinion, and who are further persecuted for standing up for defending their rights. This is evident of a serious societal failing. It's even more troubling that it takes place in countries that professes to adhere to the rule of law and abide by the tenets of human rights.

XXIX

When you have a so-called "independent" investigatory body that's only able to arrive at the same biased conclusion time and again, no matter what the evidence shows, you don't need an expert to tell you that organization is a farce, and it's only objective is to give the appearance of justice being rendered.

XXX

There are things you let go, and then there are things that you should never learn to accept. Injustice should be counted amongst those things.

XXXI

If you ever wondered why corruption continues to be a scourge on society, simply observe your own complicit or neglectful behavior in matters of wrongdoing.

XXXII

We should always support and sympathize with anyone who has endured injustice of whatever variety. It's a horrible breach of a person's unassailable rights and dignity, which he/she never emotionally vacates.

XXXIII

Injustice isn't a kin to heartache, so time won't make it good again. Nor will injustice be canceled out by a requital of recognition of the offense, or an apology in any form. Even so, the aforesaid goes a considerable distance to make amends.

XXXIV

It takes a terrible visit from injustice for one to truly understand why the words "fighting for" are most commonly used in combination with "justice." That's because Justice, strangely enough, is never granted as it should be. Instead it requires the injured person to go to battle only to incur even more scars.

XXXV

It's amazing what horrors can transpire when a society decides to deviate from common decency and disregard their own laws; and conform to sadistic practices that abuse innocent people in the name of "security," or whatever guise.

XXXVI

Wherever there's injustice you can be sure there'll be an appearance by Justification, rationalization, deflection, and deception, and of course cover-up.

XXXVII

Any citizen who fights with his/her fellow citizens on behalf (or at the behest) of any government, is essentially fighting against him/her self.

XXXVIII

Injustice has a way of activating the activist warrior gene in its victims.

—Heart Facts—

I

Every woman has already found her prince charming and every man his princess fascinating; the problem is he/she just didn't come in the package to their liking.

II

No matter how boundless someone's love is for you, if they can't be themselves around you — that fiercely burning flame will be extinguished by the fear of judgment and disapproval in your eyes.

III

Staying in a contentious relationship (or place) is like eating expired food, the toxicity may not always be visible from the surface — but you know it's there. So the earlier you can exit an ailing situation — do so forthwith.

IV

People often stay in poor relationships far longer than they should, and at the expense of future unions.

—Verses for Humanity—

I

Any practice that violates humans (or just plain decency, for that matter) should not be a part of any country's custom. It's as uncomplicated as that.

II

We must be very careful as a society not to regress on matters of civil rights and human rights. At the same time we must be equally mindful not to progress into a dystopian society.

III

It's more important to be proud of your interaction with your fellow human beings than to be tied to some obstinate loyalty to your national assignment. Your birth place is purely circumstantial and you didn't have a hand in it, after all.

IV

Governments don't confer human rights; these are natural rights that are bestowed by the creator.

V

Your human rights are *non-negotiable no matter where you are.*

—Self Notes—

I

The coveted riches to be sought should be knowledge of self and the world around you. Poverty of the mind is an affliction that affects both the rich and the deprived, equally.

II

Don't be in any haste to become an evolved person in an ever devolving world.

III

A principled person's integrity is not interdependent on other people's behavior/actions, in order for it to be present. That's because decent folks are consistent in all matters relating to honorable conduct — and not only at select times.

IV

We all will falter at some juncture — that's a given. So the issue isn't about being without fault, or about the infractions we commit against another person. Rather, it's about our ability to make the required amends when we have harmed others.

V

For many, their integrity is always on the auction block. Hence the highest bidder will always rule their world.

VI

The challenge for all of us is to cultivate a true understanding of ourselves, and then listen to our own inner voice for guidance.
A well calibrated mental compass will always ensure us a safe passage through the capricious seas of life.

VII

We are all a divine sovereignty unto ourselves, and as such we have the right to guard against intentional and unwarrantable interference into our personal affairs by any individual or entity.

VIII

When you don't know who you are, there will be no shortage of folks willing to tell you... And you know what? If you are feeble of mind, you'll believe them.

IX

When it concerns your rights it's necessary for you to be an absolutist.

X

Sometimes it isn't "just you," and instead it's everyone else. And in these moments you need to "stand up for your rights and not be humble.

XI

Honest men stand alone while dishonest men simply cower in the crowd.

XII

Stand firm in your truth, no matter how big or strong the opposition.

XIII

View any form of intrusion into your life as a threat to your ambitions and sovereignty. Then, consign all unsolicited advice about your life into the virtual trash can.

XIV

Be careful who you lend an ear, because they're liable to control your mind.

XV

Knowing your worth is how you'll ultimately be valued.

Part Two

Unsorted Musings & Maxims

1.

Ah, mockery — the intellectually poor man's favorite method of attack.

2.

The murder of the mind happens first, long before the last breath is taken.

3.

If you're too busy being haunted by ghosts from your past; you might just miss the existing folks looking to cause you harm — the present-day evil souls sitting on your doorstep.

4.

Don't let making allowances for foolish people weary you.

5.

It's okay to be the joke, just not the punch line.

6.

False humility is worse than genuine arrogance.

7.

Once you start yielding to crap of any variety, it becomes a habit.

8.

Don't be intimidated by anyone's education; instead be inspired by their accomplishments. There is a surplus of educated clowns in the world, enough to start scores of circuses.

9.

The savior of any man's sanity lies in knowing who he/she is at all times.

10.

When the unsolicited analysis of you is concluded, just make sure that you remain unchanged.

11.

A society in which avowed law abiding folks are willing to collude together in order to destroy an innocent person, is a far more dangerous place than a war-zone. For in a war-zone, there is no confusion as to who one's enemy is.

12.

The amount of pain people are willing to inflict on others is in exact measure to their own inner turmoil.

13.

A toxic society doesn't become so by chance. It is achieved through years of careful cultivation.

14.

Justification serves to excuse the behavior of the perpetrator, whilst re-injuring the victim through invalidation.

15.

If you're able to advance past all the conditioning and indoctrination, perpetrated against you over time — intentionally and unintentionally — nothing will be out of reach for you to comprehend. And, the truth will reveal itself to you in great abundance.

16.

No matter how well-meaning your intentions are; never attempt to offer advice to anyone without having a clear understanding of their situation. Otherwise, you're more apt to offend/inflict further harm, rather than render any meaningful assistance. A reputable doctor never prescribes medicine without initially examining the patient.

17.

Anyone that's imprudent enough to believe he/she has the right to direct another person's path in life is a donkey.

18.

An unanticipated revelation often makes for an uncomfortable suit.

19.

The problem with a lie is that it needs to be continually expanded, in order to retain its shape.

20.

If you care to destroy a person's argument, simply locate the logical fallacy in their reasoning. Every fallacious argument is propped-up with at least one or more misleading notions. Of course, some are more flagrant than others and therefore are much more difficult to decipher, mostly owning to the variations in the language.

21.

It's a momentous task trying to convince sheltered minds to wander beyond the meadows of their received truths and well established lies.

22.

A bought reputation soon loses its shine.

23.

Artists hate tyranny because they already serve a tyrant — their art. And as that aged refrain states; one can only attend to one master at a time.

24.

No man in good standing with his own conscience can excuse away deliberately trying to inflict pain on another human being. No matter his/her rationale.

25.

Any idiot can play games; but it calls for a genuine master to unravel a scheme.

26.

Once a lie has been lodged into a person's mind, no amount of truth can completely wipe away the deception. Therefore the remains of the falsehood become a part of their reasoning.

27.

To be united in a lie is to be ultimately divided by the insurmountable truth.

28.

You can usually tell an idiot by the things he/she is proud of.

29.

The world has always sought to make sacrificial offerings out of two sorts of people: 1) those who they deem as weak and unintelligent, and 2) those who they view as a threat — the strong & intelligent folks. Everyone else in between, the status-quo folks, will always be the least targeted.

30.

An ailing society will always seek to do to others whatever the world has done to them.

31.

The world is already running at an over-capacity level with weak people and cowards, and you should have no desire to be counted among them.

32.

Ever notice when people are nasty to you, and the moment you return fire, they're quick to put in a request for civility —and all of a sudden it's "can't we just be civil?" Your comeback to this should be: "civility" flew the coop a short time ago but if you hang around awhile "hostility" is bound to make an appearance.

33.

It's easy to attack someone from the shadows never having to defend one's animus. The wall of allusion is very thick.

34.

In order to be a teacher of others one has to first become a student of oneself. Although it's important to note that the toiling never ends, and you must put in the necessary work to become a self-integrated person.

35.

Unless you are dedicated to fully withdrawing from regular society, namely; committing to a life of monasticism, becoming an "evolved" person is mostly a futile undertaking in a chaotic world. And being an "evolved person" is like speaking in a language everyone else is unaccustomed to.

36.

The problem isn't a person's shortage of institutionalized education that hinders them; rather, it's their poor self-education that impedes their ascension.

37.

Denial is often a reflexive response in order to allay the denier from the discomfort of an undesirable truth. As well, it's an attempt by the denier to nullify the injured party's experience

38.

Dealing with people on equal terms dissolves all impediments to misunderstanding.

39.

Folks love to exclaim "no one's perfect" in defense of their often despicable violations against other people, as if the statement is a sacrament of absolution. It isn't. Rather it's an admission of guilt.

40.

Unlike a choir, the truth doesn't need any musical accompaniment to sing her song. That's because she is a brilliant soloist.

41

People tend to use "ad hominem attacks" when the facts are not on their side.

42.

It turns out that the truth is more powerful than any nuclear weapon.

43.

Folks entertain rumors about other people partly based on their own mental fractures.

44.

An atmosphere of fear and distrust is incapable of nurturing great innovators and thinkers. What it never fails to churn out however is a cadre of middling minds, folks who are only efficient at bootlegging ideas from originators. Innovation naturally requires a degree of unfettered freedom.

45.

The mass of expanded bull-crap that's created by any unjust situation tends to cloud people's mind about the victim and causes others to have a sense of suspicion about them.

46.

It's never too soon to retire from the laborious task of appeasing simple minds.

47.

Politeness can sometimes conceal a whole lot of nastiness.

48.

If someone has a problem with you, and they gripe about it to everyone else except you — then they're the problem.

49.

Cowards always attack from behind the walls of allusion.

50.

When people need you, they'll do what you want. When you need them, they'll do what they want.

51.

Selfish people will only concern themselves with you at their own convenience.

52.

Continuously offending/violating someone whilst simultaneously apologizing, immediately cancels out the request for forgiveness.

53.

The further you can see beyond the curve, or comprehend something, the less you're disposed to judge it.

54.

The repetition of a lie has never succeeded in altering a falsehood — to any degree.

55.

I believe every society has its share of aberration; that is a part of the natural composition of any place. Then there are those societies that are so tied to sadistic practices that veer far beyond the usual peculiarities of most places.

56.

Like a house that's built on granite, a life that's constructed on a sturdy base, no matter how hard the rain falls, and the flood rises, and the wind blows and thumps against it, it will not falter.

57.

All conscious writers have an extra pair of invincible ears and eyes.

58.

When you live according to what's in fashion, you have to adjust to suit the season —or risk being off trend. Alternatively, when your path in life is dictated by your own individual style (truth), you are more apt to influence aspirational tendencies in others.

59.

When idiocy goes viral it's equal in nature to an out of control wildfire, and every bit as destructive.

60.

Many people possess 20/20 vision but suffer from internal/mental blindness.

61.

A good conscience will always arrest a corrupt mind and correct its ways.

62.

It's important to have a well calibrated internal compass, and to insulate oneself against all forms of conditioning and indoctrination in whatever form they may take.

63.

It's rather easy for cowards to sling mud at other people, anonymously.

64.

The variance that separates an autodidact from a college student is after a set period of indoctrination, the undergrad will graduate with their degree. In contrast the autodidact never graduates because he/she is devoted to the lasting acquisition of knowledge.

65.

The truth can neither be outrun (not even by greatest runner), or outnumbered (not even by the biggest mob).

66.

Call folks out on their misdeeds and watch them go through the five stages of grief: denial, anger, bargaining, depression & acceptance. Alas, for those unwilling to admit their wrongdoing -the cycle will repeat itself again & again.

67

Trying to humiliate others always rewards the offender by exposing their own emotional fractures.

68.

Let people believe what they will about you... and try not to make a fuss.

69.

You should never want to be even a tiny bit of debris in the storm of someone else's life, therefore you should only enter into some else's storm to lend aid — not to increase the blustery conditions.

70.

You have to first overthrow the oppressor in your head (you know that persnickety little nag that you gave permission to devalue you), if you ever wish to triumph over the tormentors and bullies outside you. The internal forces within us will always be our greatest adversary.
So stage your coup against the enemies in your head and banish those tyrants to a faraway land.

71.

There will always be some reasons for someone else to be jealous of you.

72.

The instance, you can figure people out, you become a designated enemy in their minds. And unbeknownst to you the plot to destroy you has already commenced in that person's head.

73.

Abusive people demand silence from their victims — give them the opposite.

74.

Negative people are like bug weed. They will choke your aspirations through attrition. And every time you try to make any kind of stride in life, the negative people in your life, depending on their own goals and aspirations will give you a look that says, "Who do you think you are? You must think you're special or something." It's as if wanting to make something out of your life were a crime.

What's going on in these cases is very simple — no need for scientific research here. The fact is people who don't want very much for themselves usually want far less for you. While you're aspiring for greatness, they're hoping for your demise.

75.

Sometimes there's genius in the incidental, and an unforeseen occurrence can turn out to be a wondrous thing.

76.

Institutionalized education is meant to be supplementary to life's education and not the other way around.

77.

You correct bad behavior with opposing good habits.

78.

It often seems as if institutionalized education is requisite for fluency in unoriginality and human stupidity.

79.

Your dreams are freely and entirely your own.

80.

An intelligent person recognizes the importance of being in possession of both sides of a story, if he/she is to come to any sort of fair and reasonable conclusion. Even someone with only a single neuron left in their brain would conclude precisely the same. It doesn't require any specialized knowledge to understand this concept — just practical sense. Of course, if one is only seeking to confirm their own bitter biases — and ludicrous rumors, then all the aforementioned points hardly matter.

81.

Just as no one is perfect, neither is any place — those are self-evident facts. However, just like certain people, some places are shoddier than others, for reasons that are both specific and unique to the nature of the person and the place.

82.

Telling someone to be "humble" conveys the same meaning in every language: Let me have my way with you. Simply being kind to every living creature therefore has a greater value. Kindness places no expectations on the beneficiary in the interest of the donor. Being humble meanwhile, demands that you dim your lamp out of some misguided sense of regard for someone else, or according to some societal decree.

83.

Depression can be expressed as being void of the desire for activities that typically delight you; oppression in contrast can be summed up as being restricted from extracting pleasure from the things that interest you by an authoritarian state or from an entity that claims dominion over you.

84.

A poor player can have all the right cards and still lose, just as easily as a great player can have all the wrong cards and still be victorious. Ultimately it's all about how you play, isn't it?

85.

Here are four simple principles (you can even say these are obvious tenets) to adhere in order to be in good standing with your fellow human beings:

I. If you're intimate with someone, it should remain between you and that person.

II. If you borrow money from someone, you should repay at your earliest opportunity.

III. If you offend someone, you should apologize at once and make amends.

IV. If you're unable to receive love from someone, in the way that reflects your needs, you should bid them adieu.

86.

The attainment of mastery is determined by the desire of the mind and soul, not by institutions. There are a great many who manage to stumble out of the finest universities, but are nothing more than recitalists of received "truths"; indoctrinated beings blindly devoted to convention and traditions, and for whom the ability to think without expressed instruction is an impossibility on any given day.

87.

If you are already starting with the proposition that a person is one way or the other, chances are you will arrive at that conclusion. Hence it is best to start off with a dispassionate premise.

88.

As it is with any industry, the bottom line is money. Alas, when people are the commodity like they are in some prisons and in the mental health care system, in order to satisfy the profit gods (and control people), the rush to criminalize and institutionalize becomes the first and primary consideration. And, many innocent people are merely regarded as nothing more than sacrificial profit cows.

89.

The father of your poor decision is the son of your discontent.

90.

Once the content of a man's heart has been corrupted, it will manifest itself through the functionality of his/her mind, which will then reveal itself in his/her behavior.

91.

For every platitude that's uttered from the mouths of intelligent men and women, a brain cell dies.

92.

Brainwashed people don't think for themselves, they function according to their conditioning.

93.

Exercise your mind; don't just let it lie dormant, as if it were a doormat.

94.

I suppose everybody should think their country is the best, however, they should never believe it.

95.

Shorthand for some overused words & terms

I. Nice = oh please like me

II. Humble = let me have my way with you

III. Obedience = never question anyone in authority even if it's at your own detriment

IV. I wouldn't change a thing because it made me who I am = despite the difficulties I went through, I have gained no insights

V. It takes two to tango = although I fucked up, you're responsible for me doing what I did

VI. She's pretty for a dark skin girl = she's an exception

96.

It should be made mandatory by the decree of every black mother and father, that their sons should obtain a law degree. And I don't mean to imply they have to use the damn thing as a vocation (unless of course it's under the directive of their own heart, as I believe people should do what kindles their inner flame, and not be directed by parental/societal dictate), but more so as a necessary tool to navigate through life in suspicious societies that still assesses them as a threat that needs to be contained for the great good of society.

97.

If you are illiterate to what freedom means, then you may be inclined to believe you have it in abundance, even when you're in bondage.

98.

Just because things didn't develop the way you'd hoped in a particular situation, doesn't mean you made the wrong decision.

99.

Anyone living consciously is going to question the world.

100.

The inherent danger that accompanies standing up against an enemy force, registers low on the scale when weighed against the death sentence that comes with failing to act in the presence of evil.

101.

The idea of trying to beat-down a man or woman whilst simultaneously placing oneself in the role of their savior is far from being a novel idea. It's actually the stock and trade of all duplicitous scoundrels.

102.

Most people will go to war with a person who damages their property. However, if they are personally violated in some way — they are far more disposed to "let it go." And it's exactly this sort of imprudent attitude that's the reason why the majority of folks' properties are in a better condition than they are.

103.

Whenever you confront privileged, entitled folks, who view themselves as being above reproach (and you as not being quite worthy of regard), you often get the same redirection of immaterial facts and skewed statistics about ones' ethnic group as a way to reassign blame. It's a failsafe response you can expect from folks of this ilk no matter the occasion.

104.

Respect and love gained through coercion is like counterfeit products made from inferior material meant to mimic the real thing, because even though it may have the air of genuineness, it's only a poor imitation.

105.

Insecure people judge and project; secure people reflect and correct.

106.

Never give credence to anyone who can publicly criticize another country or ethnic group, but is unable to do the same with his/her motherland and own kinfolk. There is no need for a doctor's visit to determine that this person suffers from a grave case of ethnocentrism, and sees primacy in his/her own race.

107.

Always let the sound your enemy hears from you be the uproarious vibration from your ascension and not the augury of your defeat.

108.

Fighting an anonymous source — even a known one — is like engaging in combat with a ghost. Or perhaps "shadow boxing" is a more fitting term.

109.

When you're created from kingly stock, neither time, nor banks of fools can depreciate your value.

110.

Atmosphere is to a creative person what hot air from an oven is to a cake. If the searing heat is not appropriately circulated throughout the oven, the cake will not rise properly. In the same way, if an artist occupies an environment that's not favorable to the circumstances of his/her nature, he/she will be less productive.

111.

Artists are merely the lowly holders of the mirror; you are responsible for the images you see of yourself.

112.

It's not law that makes just men; it's being the proprietor of a well-adjusted conscience.

113.

A real artist is like a selfish lover, that is to say, he/she is concerned with securing their own release first and foremost. In other words everyone else is subordinate to the creative process. So creatively speaking, all artists are selfish lovers.

114.

You know you're a writer like you know when you're in love. The feelings are exactly the same; you are consumed by your passion, you can't wait to be alone with your thoughts, and you'll do anything for your creative muse.

115.

A Smear campaign is designed to remove the responsibility off the perpetrator and assign the blame to their victim.

116.

The lesson one can expect to receive from standing up to corrupt folks is that they will say or do any and everything to justify their actions. The fact is these ethically compromised folks are the same make and model of people as criminals.

117.

Any country that would contravene their own laws can't really be expected to respect their citizens.

118.

Even when we sometimes lack the superficial niceties of everyday life, we should still endeavor to be infinitely kind to all living things.

119.

Only a jester tries to offer advice for a situation they lack knowledge about.

120.

Far too often people get discombobulated by the whys and the wherefores. Why would they do that? Why wouldn't they do this? This is exactly the sort of reckless argument that has caused the ruination of a lot of innocent people, even got a great many killed. The fact is people will do some evil and abominable things in order to conceal their deceptions.

121.

Your humility should be held in reserve for those less-fortunate. Meanwhile, you should direct the swindlers of humanity and the corrupt folks sitting on high and casting their stones down low to choke on your conceit, perpetually.

122.

Just as it's important to comport oneself with grace and dignity in certain matters, the opposite is required when the situation calls for it.

123.

I firmly believe what many persons brand as "karma," is nothing more than a malicious cycle of emotionally injured and disturbed people projecting their misery onto other folks.

124.

Most people shower every day, but it's their "mind and soul" that are in dire need of a proper washing.

125.

No one is ever going to give you an accurate valuation of yourself. So why even bother soliciting others' opinion.

126.

It's counterproductive to insulate yourself with prejudicial behaviors such as class, race, age, etc.

127.

Happiness may elude you on occasion, being the abstract creature that she/he is, – even so, never permit it to get in the way of your contentment – not even in the midst of life's storms.

128.

Many people naively believe "happiness" is a destination you arrive at — it isn't. Instead, happiness runs along a continuum with varying degrees of joy and sadness, and as such, it's not a permanent state of being that can ever be achieved.

129.

Lately, there seems to be a new strain of ignorance that's far more resistant to practical sense. Then again, perhaps it's always been with us, and it's just been lying dormant for the last century, or so.

130.

An English teacher is no more a brilliant writer than a sports coach is a great athlete. The reason for this is obvious; they both require separate skill sets.

131.

One has to adapt to the circumstances of the weather, no matter how severe it gets, after all — it's Mother Nature,–and there's no contest. On a contrary note, one should never acclimate to a toxic environment — or bear a moment of indignity for the misery of being in a dispiriting milieu.

132.

The Invaluable Benefits of Practicing Contemplation

Contemplation is akin to a force; one that immerses you into the realm of your intellectual and spiritual superior self. In the state of contemplation you are activated, present, reflective, observant, and locked into the sacred source of your being. Thus you are naturally disposed and primed to obtain unadulterated knowledge and guidance at a loftier frequency.

133.

Entrepreneurs: If you believe in the beauty and wonder of your idea/product, make it at a loss (if you have to), until you can make it at a profit. Most importantly though,–Never Give up on Your Dreams.

134.

When it comes to crimes against humanity, human rights violations, injustice and corruption; we should never sit idly by with our lips sealed in the face of such transgressions.

135.

I believe when people lack comprehension about a particular thing, they're disposed at a higher degree to take whatever is offered to them as facts, for the most part because their mind needs someplace to rest. And, because they've assigned truth to their belief, even a falsehood starts to bear a resemblance to reality.

If you're reading these parting remarks, valued reader, I will deduce that you've read the entire book from beginning to end. I would now like to pose the following suppositions about your experience:
1) you either found the book pleasantly engrossing (or perhaps only mildly interesting enough to wade through to the end),
— or
2) you are just the sort of person who always finishes what you start,
— or
3) the book bored you in to a tailspin and you simply skipped to end to read this annotation to see what additional pain I would I inflict on you.

If the latter was your answer to the preceding statements, accept my heartfelt apology and you have my permission to gift the book to your favorite adversary. In the event the former is how this collection registered in your heart, I hope you will endorse the book to your cadre of acquaintances — and give it a space on your bookshelf.

Regards,
Hendrick

Notes & Sources

1. Several pieces included in this collection, specifically the ones about dreams and triumphing over odds, were lifted from other works by the author, namely — the book "The Music I Love, The Business I Hate," with a few small tweaks here and there.

2. Some previously published piece on social media were also included as part of this collection.

3. The entire cluster of musings and maxims were composed while the author was living under extreme political/personal persecution; first in the Bahamas — and then Canada.

4. All the material in this book both fresh as well as formerly publicized pieces were written solely by the author.